What Readers Say About

When Angels Touch You

L.C. Hayden's book will help you see the angels waiting to be invited into your life. Her book is as friendly as an invitation to a Texas barbecue—but the neighbors in her book are angelic.

The Rev. Mary O'Gara, D.D.
New Mexico

Inspiring, heartwarming, tear jerking—this book left me spiritually uplifted, renewed my faith, and gave me confidence in the power of miracles.

Kate Wiederkehr
University Student
Texas

I found myself wanting to talk to the author because as I was reading the book, I felt the narrative draw me in.

Teri Davis
Teacher
Nebraska

In When Angels Touch You, *L.C. Hayden reveals a real depth of faith as she inspires us with stories of angels who influence her circumstances. Very intriguing!*

Mary F. Albert
High School Librarian
Texas

I recommend this thought-provoking book. It will make you think back to incidents that have happened in your own life. Maybe there was an angel or two there. I learned many things about angels that I didn't know.

Donna Kaster
Retired
Arizona

When Angels Touch You

by

L.C. Hayden

Hey Marlene -
- may the angels
touch you!
Take care,
LC Hayden

When Angels Touch You

ISBN 1-932196-01-3

P.O. Box 1785
Georgetown, Texas 78627

Printed in the United States of America

This book is dedicated to all of the Bolds
with lots and lots of love:

In West Virginia:
J and Vickie Bolds
Sarah Bolds

In Massachusetts:
Jamé and Jennifer Bolds

In Florida:
Michele Bolds

Acknowledgments

I know of no book ever written without the help of many people. This book is no exception. Several people read the early drafts and suggested changes, offered ideas, or corrected my mistakes. I'd especially like to thank Mary Albert, Vickie Bolds, Donna Kaster, Lee Taylor, and Charlene Tess.

Lots of kudos go to my brother Joe Amaro for his beautiful artwork which you will enjoy throughout this book. The only drawing not his is the one before each *About Angels* section. I am guilty of that one. Also, thanks to Joe and Alex Wiederkehr for their endless hours spent on the computer making the photographs publishable quality.

And Rich, my husband, thanks for taking that beautiful picture of the sunset in Cozumel. I know you'll enjoy the picture every time you look at the cover of my book. And Rich, thanks for all of your support, love, and advice. Thanks also to Don and Robert, our sons. Thank you for being you. You all are my special angels.

I'd also like to thank my editor, publisher, and friends, Joan R. Neubauer and her husband Steve, for all they've done to make this dream a reality.

But above all, I'd like to thank God for sending me His angels to guide me and protect me. Without Him, I'd be nothing.

About Angels

Be not forgetful to entertain strangers: for thereby some have entertained angels unawares.

Hebrews 13:2

Behold, I send an Angel before thee, to keep thee in the way, and to bring thee into the place which I have prepared.

Exodus 23:20

For He shall give His angels charge over thee, to keep thee in all thy ways.

Psalm 91:11

The Bible mentions angels three hundred times, while Jesus referred to them fifteen times. Open your heart and let an angel in.

Foreword

Some people live enchanted lives. The rest of us just seem to drag along. We spend our days expecting Murphy's Law to slap us in the face. Soon we see our lives filled with nothing but mishap. But then, that's how life goes, right?

Wrong.

I'm living proof that life doesn't have to unfold that way. Not only are we entitled to hope for miracles, the Bible tells us that we have every right to expect them to happen to us. But just exactly how will these miracles manifest themselves? Who will orchestrate them?

Enter angels.

When we invite them into our lives, they mediate between us humans and God. The word *angel* comes from the Greek word *angelos*, meaning *messengers*. As such, they stand with us when we're depressed or lonely. They come to us when we find ourselves in danger. They provide comfort. They teach us and protect us.

Often, we will see them as other human beings. And why not? They can be either male or female. They can take on the nationality or race for which the circumstances dictate. More often than not, we are unaware of their presence. We simply stand awed by the miracles they perform.

They often go unthanked as we attribute the miracle to a stroke of good luck, or a coincidence. But let me assure you, angels stand by us and cause miracles to unfold.

The more we heighten our awareness of the angels that surround us, the more we allow them into our lives, and the easier it will be for these angels to mediate between us and God.

With this premise in mind, I invite you to journey with me through the glorious land of miracles. Each of the following true incidents will show you how my life has been enriched and how, in turn, your life can grow and change *When Angels Touch You.*

Word Origin

The word *angaros* in Persian means courier. From the Hebrew language we get the term *malakh* which means *messenger*. Both of these words define the angels' primary function: they listen to our prayers, carry them to heaven, and bring God's answer back to us.

Miracle 1

The Beginning

A coin purse.

It was just a simple coin purse with a zipper top. Surely I could see nothing outstanding about it and it was certainly not expensive. But for me this plain coin purse became the symbol of my maturity. I had now graduated to the fourth grade. Surely I had left my childhood behind and had become this more mature, responsible girl.

That's not how my mom saw me.

"Why do you want that coin purse? All you're going to do is lose it like you lose everything," she said.

I bit my lip. Not this time. I would hold on to this wallet forever-and-a-day. My mom would then recognize that I indeed had blossomed into a mature young lady.

The author, as a child, trying to act grownup.

My mom handed me the coin holder, and I stuffed my dollar into it. This constituted my entire life's savings, lunch money for the week. I would guard that coin purse with my life. I gathered my books and headed for school.

The teacher taught us all about George Washington, adjectives and adverbs, and long division. I stuffed my hand in my pocket, wanting to feel the symbol of my maturity. My hand reached all the way down to the bottom of my empty pocket.

A lump the size of a lemon formed in my throat. Surely, the coin purse hadn't vanished. I must have dropped it when I sat down. It had to be on the floor, right down there by my feet.

I glanced down.

Nothing.

Without attracting the teacher's attention, I looked around on the floor. Nothing there. Could it be under my desk? As best as I could, I swept the area with my foot. Still no luck.

"You will have ten minutes to do your arithmetic work." The teacher headed back to her desk. "Show your work and turn in your paper when you're finished."

Great news. That meant I could get up and search for my coin purse. I got down on all fours and looked under my desk. Nothing. Surely, under the desk in front of me, it would be there. But it wasn't. I couldn't find it under the desk behind me, or under the one beside me, or kitty-corner from me. I searched by the pencil sharpener.

I retraced my steps. Had I shown my prized possession to anyone? Yes, I had flaunted it to everyone. The bell rang and I stuffed it in my pocket. I distinctly remembered doing that. But could I have placed it in my coat pocket instead of my pants' pocket?

New hope sprung within me as I dashed

toward the back of the room where I had hung my coat beside those of my classmates. I reached deep into the right pocket. The left pocket. Disappointment ate at me when I realized that they too were empty.

Sure, I felt drained, but I refused to give up. Maybe when I placed my coat on the hook, the coin purse fell down. I looked, but like before, no luck.

Tears stung my eyes as I headed back to my desk. I'd never see the wallet again. My mom had been right. I was just an irresponsible little kid.

I went back to my desk, finished my work, and rechecked every inch of the room, left to right and front to back. My search, as before, proved to be fruitless.

I looked out the window, up toward the irresistible blue sky. "God," I said, "please help me find my wallet."

It had been a simple prayer whispered in childish innocence. I turned my attention back to my work. But not for long.

My thoughts strayed toward the lost coin purse. Search one more time, my inner voice told me. I glanced down at the floor. There, by my feet, lay a folded piece of paper. Had it always been there? I didn't remember seeing it.

I unfolded it. Someone had written the following letters: A T B O T R U T C. I didn't read it as letters. The code shouted at me as clearly as if it had been written in longhand. I knew what it said: at the back of the room under the coats.

I've already checked there. I thought. I'll be wasting my time and I didn't need empty hope. But this note. . .this note. . .

I stood up, headed toward the back of the classroom, and looked on the floor. There it was, under the coats.

I picked up my coin purse.

I don't remember if I checked to see if my dollar was still there. That didn't matter. I had the important part.

Unfortunately, I no longer have the wallet or the note. Had I realized the significance of my find, I would have cherished them for the rest of my life.

Not only did I gain something very valuable that day, I also lost something. Being a child, I didn't recognize the importance of my find. The memory got pushed into the innermost recesses of my mind, and there it would lie dormant for many years to come.

Raziel

Have you ever wondered who keeps the secrets of the Universe? That would be the angel Raziel. His name means either *Secrets of God* or *Angel of Mystery*.

Miracle 2

God's Mysterious Ways

Like everyone else, I left my childhood behind and blossomed into that dreadful stage: I became a teenager. Being a typical teen, I took everything for granted. At that time, the miraculous things that happened had nothing to do with miracles. Instead, just like most people, I thought of them as either coincidences or lucky breaks.

My most memorable break began in the summer between my junior and senior year of high school when I met a young man by the name of Richard Lloyd Hayden, my future husband.

We met in San Diego, California. He was a

sailor, bound for the United States Naval Communications Station on the island of Manila in the Philippines.

I, on the other hand, would spend my senior year at Austin High School in El Paso, Texas. We corresponded throughout my senior year, and inside one of those letters, he sent me his ring.

The flat surface of the gold-plated ring contained his initials, but that's not what I noticed first. I remember thinking how huge this ring was. In fact, huge would not adequately describe it. Now, to be fair, I must admit that I've always been on the petite side. My wedding ring is size two. His ring size hovers between eight and nine.

When I slipped the ring on, my fingers spread apart. Even so, I put yarn around the back of the ring and proudly wore it.

Time marched on, and I graduated. That summer I traveled to California with my dad, mom, my sister, Vickie, and my brother, Arts.

While riding in the car, I looked up at the road in front of me. It stretched for miles like a thin, straight, gray ribbon. The perfect blue sky spoke of no danger ahead.

I turned to my five-year old brother who

was cutting some paper with sharp scissors. "Put those scissors up," I told him.

My brother, Arts, as he looked around the time of the accident.

"Why?" he asked, a question mark stamped on his face.

Why? I had no idea why I said that, but, hey, since I'd already said it, I figured I might as well reinforce my authority. "Do it!"

He opened his carrying case and stuffed the scissors inside. He barely had a chance to snap the box shut before my mom, who had been driving, lost control of the car. It rolled over four times and eventually came to a stop, belly-side up.

I remember looking at the road and listening to my mom scream. The next thing I recollect was waking up. I undid my seat belt and fell on my head. I gasped. I hadn't realized I was hanging upside down.

I looked around. My brother was still strapped to the seat. My sister and both of my parents had been thrown from the car. Then, thankfully, my sister, crawled back in to help us.

I turned to Arts. "You're upside down," I told him. "I'm going to undo your seat belt, and you'll fall down. Don't be afraid, okay?"

He nodded, his eyes, like two huge balls on his face. I released him and Vickie and I helped him crawl out.

As he wiggled his way out of the car, I heard my dad gasp, "Elsie!"

"I'm okay, Daddy," I said. "I'm just helping Arts get out."

My dad's sigh of relief told me all I needed to know. Everyone—thank God—had survived the accident with only minor injuries.

By the time I crawled out of the car, people had stopped and offered help. The driver of an eighteen-wheeler offered us the use of his truck to change out of our bloody clothes. I would have accepted his kind offer except that our luggage lay scattered all over the road. Most of the suitcases opened on impact and spilled their contents.

A lady—a complete stranger—offered my parents a thousand dollars to use in any way they needed, quite a hefty sum when you realize that this accident happened in 1968. A thousand dollars was worth a lot more then.

The police arrived next. They talked to my dad for a while. He explained how the accident happened as they walked toward the wreckage. I followed them.

After getting all the details, one of the policemen shook his head. "Do you folks know how lucky you are? If the car had rolled just one more time. . ." He pointed at the metal storm pipes in the median. The car had come to a stop less than a foot away from them. "If the car had rolled even a foot further, you folks would have been on top of those metal pipes. Who knows what would have happened then."

The other policeman noted another lucky break. "Not only that, look at that car." The area between the seats and the roof measured slightly more than a foot. "How you all escaped with only scratches and bruises is beyond me."

Maybe he didn't understand, but I did.

The arrival of the ambulance diverted our attention as they prepared mom and Vickie for a trip to the hospital.

As a result of the routine check, the doctors found that Vickie suffered from valley fever. Her lung collapsed and her heart was pushed to the side. Had she not been involved in that accident, she would not have been at the hospital where she could receive proper treatment.

The next day, my dad, Arts, and I went back to the site of the accident. We hoped to collect any personal items that might still have been out there.

One of the things I hoped to find was Rich's ring. Somehow, during the accident the ring had fallen off, even though the yarn I had placed around the back of the ring measured at least half an inch in thickness.

We found some clothes, a pair of shoes, some make up and a few curlers.

No ring.

But I did find the yarn. It had been neatly cut in half, length-wise. Had I not been wearing that ring, I surely would have lost my finger.

And had that accident not happened, I would have lost something much more important. I could have lost my sister. But because of the accident, doctors discovered the disease early enough and my sister fully recovered.

They say God travels in mysterious ways.

I couldn't agree more.

Raphael

The Archangel Raphael, the patron of travelers, healers, and fishermen, is also the angel of knowledge and science. He also defends women who have been falsely accused. He is considered the patron of lovers and the blind.

Miracle 3

An Awakening

All the minor injuries I suffered from the car accident healed nicely, and gradually, I pushed the memory of what had happened to the darker recesses of my mind. I knew I had been blessed with many miracles during that accident and I felt grateful. But I wasn't quite ready to acknowledge them as such. What I needed was a miracle to slap me in the face—and that's exactly what the next one did.

"There he goes again," Rich told me. He pointed to the white truck pulling a horse trailer.

I giggled. We had been playing tag down

Highway 40 for the last hour. We had now left Memphis behind us and were heading toward West Virginia to where Vickie and her husband, J Bolds had moved.

I watched the white truck as it passed us. Most of the time, he was either the vehicle directly in front of us or behind us.

"Just watch me," Rich said. "Within the next few minutes, we'll be in front again."

That never happened.

Our engine died.

Suddenly and totally without any warning, it just gave out.

I gasped. "What happened?"

The cars behind us honked.

Rich got out and pushed the car to the side. Cars zoomed by. He opened the hood and stared at the engine.

"Can you fix it?" My thoughts strayed to our limited budget. What would we have to give up in order to pay the repair bill?

"I'm not sure. I don't see anything wrong with it."

Rich's background in auto mechanics has always been limited so his answer didn't surprise me. "Any suggestions?"

He shook his head. No matter how long we

stared at the dead engine, that wouldn't help fix it. "Go try to start the car. Maybe I can spot something wrong."

I prayed he could. I got in and turned the key. Nothing. No click. No spark. Not even the grinding noise of the engine. What a bummer.

"I guess we should lock it and walk to the nearest gasoline station." Rich closed the hood.

Cell phones hadn't been invented yet, and we didn't have a C.B. radio. We were on our own.

I knew we had just left West Memphis, and I tried to recall how far back we'd have to walk. From where we stood, we couldn't see a single gasoline station.

"Let me grab my purse, and then we can head back."

Rich got in the car, too. "Let's give it one more try before we start walking."

I knew nothing would happen. A dead engine couldn't simply come to life. "Sure." I tried to make my tone sound hopeful.

Rich hesitated and we made small talk, while we both focused our minds on our unfortunate situation. Five minutes dragged by.

"I guess we'd better be heading out." Rich looked out the window, back toward the city. "I just want to give it one more try before we take off."

I nodded, reaching for my purse.

The engine purred just as it would after having a major tune up. Rich's eyes popped open like two huge, round buttons. Not a single indicator light lit up. "It's working." His voice came out as a low whisper as though filled with disbelief. "None of the gauges indicate anything wrong."

I couldn't think of what to say. If the car performed perfectly fine right now, why had it stopped fifteen minutes ago? I asked the first thing that popped into my mind. "Should we turn back or keep heading forward?"

Rich considered the possibilities. "Let's keep going. We'll keep our eyes peeled for a gas station if it becomes necessary."

We blended in with the traffic. Our car maneuvered beautifully, never once giving any indication that it had malfunctioned just a little while ago.

We hadn't driven far when traffic came to an abrupt stop.

We reasoned that up ahead, there must either be construction, or worse, a car accident. We hoped for the construction, but doubted it since we hadn't seen any signs indicating construction on the road ahead of us.

As with all traffic jams, we creepy-crawled along, and at times we, along with the rest of the cars, stood at a standstill. We worried that our engine would overheat, and the car would once again stall.

That never happened.

Half an hour later we could see the reason for the traffic jam: a major pile up. There must have been at least ten cars involved in the accident. As we neared it, we could see a little better. One of the cars involved was the white truck pulling the horse trailer. Had our car not died, we would have been part of that horrible accident.

The hairs on the back of my neck stood up and a chill ran down my spine. I understood why our car had died. I whispered a thank you to God for sending His angels to protect us.

Significant Subject

The editors of *Encyclopedia Britannica* were asked to select the 102 most significant subjects of western thought. Their first entry? Angels, of course.

Miracle 4

The Voice from Above

The days passed and the "car-won't-start incident" became nothing more than a story we'd repeat at family gatherings or parties. Time marched on and by now Rich and I had become parents to two wonderful boys, Don and Robert. Summer had arrived which meant vacation time. This particular season, we again chose to travel to West Virginia to visit the Bolds.

We'd been cramped in the car the entire day, so when we reached the outskirts of Scott Depot, West Virginia, we all let out a sigh of relief.

Soon Don and Robert would be playing

with Jamé and Michele, our nephew and niece, while the adults settled back for a nice, relaxed conversation.

That lasted no more than ten minutes.

"You've had a chance to unwind from your driving." Vickie shifted positions as though she felt uncomfortable. "Before you get too settled in, we need to tell you. Uncle Bill called. Aunt Marie passed away yesterday. The funeral is tomorrow."

Aunt Marie, our favorite aunt, dead.

Impossible.

We decided to head out. Since we all wouldn't fit in one car, the Bolds took their car, and we drove ours. We left immediately because we knew we'd have to drive the twenty-four hours straight through if we expected to reach Van Alstyne, Texas, in time for the funeral.

Because the news of Aunt Marie's death hung on me like an albatross, Rich took the first shift and drove until 2:00 in the morning. I sat in the passenger seat and forced myself to stay awake. Rich and I carried on a conversation, talking about everything and nothing. I felt I had to talk to him so he wouldn't fall asleep.

Mistake number one.

True, I managed to keep him awake, but I didn't get a chance to sleep. When I switched from the passenger's seat to the driver's seat, I felt sleep's embrace wrap its tentacles around me. I shook it off and began the drive.

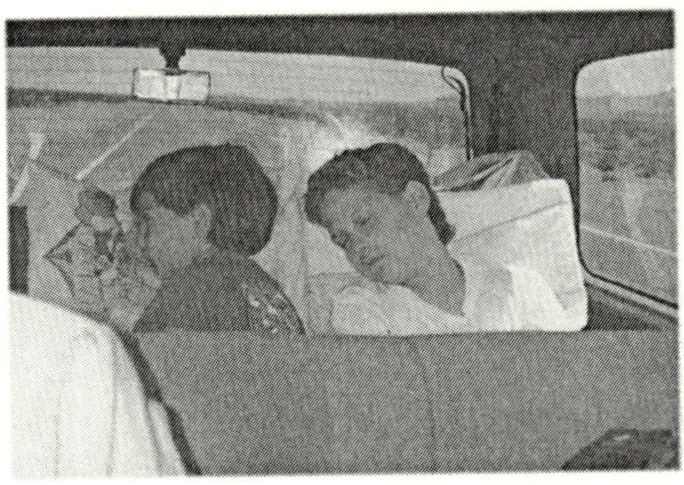

Robert (left) and Don (right) get comfortable and prepare to sleep during the long drive.

At first, Vickie and I kept up a fairly good conversation over the C.B. radio. By now, we had learned the importance of having one of those radios. We're no dummies.

As the minutes dragged on, our conversation became more forced than spontaneous. Soon we both gave up the idea of trying to talk to each other. We both simply felt too tired to talk.

Mistake number two.

About an hour later, sleep once again beckoned me.

I rolled down the window.

It didn't help.

I turned on the radio.

I tapped the steering wheel, keeping rhythm to the music.

I had triumphed. Sleep and I had struggled for control, and I had won—or so I thought.

I distinctly heard a voice right next to my right ear say, "Wake up!"

My eyes snapped open.

In what must have been the few seconds I closed my eyes, I had steered the car away from the pavement, past the shoulder, and toward the incline. My heart jumped to my throat as I straightened the car just in time.

The incident had startled me enough to drive away all desire to sleep. My wide-awake senses told me something magical had happened. Someone had whispered the urgent message in my ear. Yet, when I looked around, my husband and my children were sound asleep. No one in that car had urged me to wake up.

Yet, someone did.

The voice had been neither male nor female. It had just been a voice.

A voice from above.

Studying Angels

If you want to impress your scholarly friends, tell them that you are an angelologist, one who studies angelology, the study of angels.

Miracle 5

A Working Angel?

Even though several years had passed, I often thought of that voice. That led me to wonder about my Guardian Angel. Had my angel ever made an earthly appearance? Had it been a male or a female one? Had he chosen to be tall or short?

It certainly didn't matter. I thrive in the knowledge that God had sent His angels to protect me. Any time I feel discouraged or confused, I simply recall the incident, and I feel warm all over. Always, that is, except for one particular Saturday morning in early May.

Anger raged within me, encompassing everything and everyone. No one, not even my Guardian Angel, would be spared my claws of fury.

For the last couple of weeks I had been watching the weeds in our front yard grow. I asked Rich and both of the boys to pull them, but they didn't. Other things much more important had to be done.

I knew that I'd end up doing that chore, as well as the laundry. . . cleaning the house. . . buying the groceries. . .balancing the budget. . . I'd have to do it all by myself. And now, add to this growing list, yard work.

What a bummer.

Since the summer temperatures in El Paso can make an oven feel like a dessert oasis, I knew the best time to perform this task would be early in the morning. On that particular Saturday—the only day I could sleep in late and relax—I set the alarm clock to go off at six. I sprang out of bed and immediately started to work.

After what seemed an eternity, I glanced at my watch. Only two hours had crept by and I already felt hot and tired. With each weed I pulled, the fury within me burned deeper. Rich, Don, and Robert were inside the house, sound asleep in the cool comfort of the air conditioner. I, on the other hand, had perspiration covering every inch of my body. My muscles ached as I strained them while fighting a weed that refused to relinquish its grasp on life.

There's no such thing as a guardian angel, I said to myself as I wiped sweat from my brow. *If there were angels, I wouldn't be here by myself pulling out these horrible weeds. My angel would be down here with me, pulling out the weeds right next to me.*

My thoughts strayed to Michael Landon's television series *Highway to Heaven*. Isn't that what he, as an angel, would have done?

I giggled at the idea of an angel actually coming down to pull weeds. I felt better and giggled some more. The giggle froze in my throat.

The first thing I saw were the shoes. Normal shoes, but shoes I didn't recognize. Someone stood beside me, so close, almost to the point of invading my private space.

Normally I'm a friendly person. I smile and greet people. Not this time. I continued to work, pretending no one stood beside me.

Then he did the most unnatural thing. He bent down and started pulling out weeds. If I had been shaken up before, now I felt completely stunned. Still, I could not fully look at him, although I did manage to sneak one quick glance.

He concentrated on the task at hand, his head bent low. He seemed short for a man, standing maybe five feet five, five-six. I believe he wore black frame glasses—does this mean he wasn't a perfect angel? He was Oriental.

Introduce yourself, my mind shouted at me. *Or at least ask him what he's doing*. That's silly. I knew what he was doing. What I really wanted to know was why he was doing it.

I opened my mouth to form the question. The words got caught in my throat and refused to come out. Okay then, at least thank him. Or ask him if he wants a glass of juice. Or milk. Or payment.

Still my mouth refused to cooperate.

Here in El Paso, most of the weeds grow deep roots, as they must dig their way through the uncaring earth to reach the almost non-existent water. I found such a weed. Lucky me. I dug around it.

As I fought with this weed, my mind continued to concentrate on my mysterious friend. This time I would swallow my anxiety and talk to him. Instead, I continued to dig. *At least mention the weather*, I told myself. A brilliant line like “It’s hot, isn’t it?” would open the door to conversation.

Normally, I don’t have a problem with being shy, and I’m certainly not a rude person. Really. I continued to dig. I pulled and dug, and the weed almost gave in.

Quit peediddling, I ordered myself. *Do it*. I swallowed hard, and prepared myself to acknowledge him. I turned, only to find that I was alone. I looked up and down the street. No one was there.

He had vanished as swiftly as he had arrived.

So, wherever you are, thank you for helping me weed my yard, but more important, thank you for letting me know You are there.

Again.

Always.

Your Weekly Angels

So today is Monday. Is there a particular angel who is responsible for that day? Sure. In fact, each day of the week has a chief angel.

Monday: Gabriel
Tuesday: Samuel
Wednesday: Raphael
Thursday: Sachiel
Friday: Anael
Saturday: Cassiel
Sunday: Michael.

Miracle 6

The Gift from Above

One of the lessons I learned from that miracle is that miracles don't have to be earth-shattering events, but could be something as trivial as pulling weeds. Or wishing for something. By June 2000, two of my mystery novels *Who's Susan?* and *When Colette Died* had been released. I have discovered that even though both books continue to receive great reviews, I must continuously work to promote my work.

Consequently, Rich and I set out on a promotional tour through the western and northwestern states. Since most bookstores prefer to schedule autograph sessions on weekends, that leaves Mondays through

Thursdays for sightseeing and relaxing.

On this one particular weekday, we decided to visit Dash Point State Park in Washington. We planned our visit to coincide with the arrival of low tide. I marveled at the beauty of life. Starfish of various colors and sizes captivated my interest.

Seeing all of this life reminded me of our scuba diving trips. There's nothing like floating underwater surrounded by vibrant colors and abundant life. This underwater world has always filled me with so much serenity that I wanted to capture it and take it with me wherever I went.

Don't be silly, I told myself. That's impossible. Yet, I really wanted to capture this charm and bring it home with me. I spent the next few days thinking about it, then an idea struck me.

I asked my dad, who has been gifted with artistic talent, to create an underwater diorama for me. He did, and the piece turned out to be a masterpiece of three-dimensional art. In the background, he painted a scuba diver swimming toward coral reefs created from Styrofoam and paint. Then he placed seashells, plastic fish, and bits and pieces of underwater fauna that we had found on the shores of Cozumel, into an attractive arrangement.

I knew the addition of a starfish would be perfect for my underwater diorama.

At present, Rich and I weren't in Cozumel. We were in Washington, enjoying the low tide area. My mind drifted back to the diorama. A starfish would make an ideal addition to my underwater display. However, two things prevented this wish from becoming a reality.

One, I would never kill a living organism just so I could display it in my home. Two, I had no way of transporting it back to the camper. In order to reach the low tide area, we had climbed down a hill. A fragile starfish would never make it back.

I sighed.

I really wanted a starfish.

Forget it.

We continued our walk and exploration.

So many starfish.

I hit my toe on something.

My glance traveled downward. A small, blue piece no more than a quarter inch in height protruded from the sand.

Dig. Investigate, I told myself.

I bent down, dug effortlessly around it, and uncovered a child's blue shovel—the type that kids take to the beaches along with a matching pail so that they can build their castles and play in the sand.

I looked around. Amazingly, we were the only ones at the site. We saw no little kids to ask about the shovel. I could claim it.

Okay, so now I had a way to transport the starfish. But surely, I couldn't kill a defenseless creature. Hey, wait a minute. I did remember seeing several dead starfish. They had even started to disintegrate. Maybe if I found one that was almost complete.

Hope sprung in my heart. Why else would I have found the shovel if not to make my wish come true? Problem was, I really didn't want a partial starfish. I wanted a complete, perfect starfish.

Amazing how I can be so demanding, huh? I began my quest. This starfish had three of its legs missing. No good. That one over there had most of its center missing. Ugh. This one, on the other hand, was worth considering. Most of its parts were still intact. True, portions of its legs were missing, and it had a hole in its middle. Still, that could be it.

I reached for it. I stopped. Something else had captured my attention.

Not knowing what I had seen or even where, I left my precious find knowing full well I'd never locate it again. I had nothing to mark the site, and one hole filled with salt water looked identical to the hundreds of other holes.

I followed my instincts to an area maybe

three hundred feet away. In so doing, I moved away from the low tide area and closer to the ocean. That's when I saw it.

Someone had created a circle composed of starfish. Some were big. Some small. All colorful. All beautiful. And definitely, all dead. Their legs had already started to curl upward.

I glanced over at the selection of starfish. I had approximately ten or so from which to choose. I settled on a beautiful, red one. I scooped it up with the shovel and carried it back to our campground.

I smiled all the way back, for I knew I carried my precious gift from above.

Angels and Names

Have you ever wondered if a person's name is important? Would it make a difference to God what our earthly name is? At least in one particular case, we know that God had wanted a child to be called by a particular name.

Zacharias' lot was to burn incense in the Temple of the Lord. While there, the Angel Gabriel appeared to him and told him that his wife Elizabeth would bear him a son who would be called John.

Zacharias couldn't believe the messenger as both he and his wife were up in years. As a result, the angel struck him dumb. When the child was born, friends and family gathered and expected the baby's name to be Zacharias.

Elizabeth told them she preferred the name John.

"That's hardly a traditional family name," the friends protested.

The father demanded a tablet and wrote, "His name is John," then handed it to his wife.

The baby's name officially became John, fulfilling God's wish as revealed by the angel Gabriel. Once this happened, Zacharias' voice miraculously returned.

(Luke 1:5-25, 57-64)

Miracle 7

Angels Guarding My Son

One month later, I received yet another gift from above. This time, however, I wouldn't be the sole recipient.

The incident began when my idea and my son's idea of safe transportation clashed. He loves speed, the feel of the wind, and freedom. All of these put together spell motorcycle.

Consequently, I should have anticipated his statement: "Mom, I'm buying a motorcycle."

I should have prepared myself, but I hadn't. Instead, my heart filled with fear. Even if he drove carefully, as he promised he would, what guarantee did I have that the other drivers would watch out for my son?

The accident totaled Don's first motorcycle.

I knew I'd never talk him out of buying the motorcycle. His dream had always been to own and ride one.

Fighting back all kinds of fears, Rich and I went with Don to buy his motorcycle.

"So what about the helmet?" I asked as I pointed to the display.

Don looked down. "Sorry, Mom, I can barely afford the down payment. I don't have the extra hundred dollars to buy one."

Rich and I led him to the sales department. "Choose one," I said, "and promise me that you'll never ride that motorcycle without wearing one."

Don obliged.

We watched as he strapped on the helmet, mounted the motorcycle, and rode away. The anxiety around me could have been slashed with a knife. Who's going to watch out for him? The sense of foreboding deepened. I whispered a prayer for him.

Gradually, the hours turned to days, and the days turned to weeks. Even though I had grown accustomed to the idea of my then twenty-two year old son riding his motorcycle, each time he walked out of the house, the knot of anxiety thickened in my stomach.

Then one day I stepped into his bedroom. I felt my mouth dry up as if it had been stuffed with cotton. My arms and legs trembled. There, on top of his dresser, rested the practically new helmet. He wasn't wearing it!

"Why, Don?" I asked him once he returned.

"I don't like it. It restricts my view. It's bothersome."

My fears blossomed once again. I couldn't force him to wear it. Who was going to watch out for him? The answer came as a whisper in the wind. "I will," the voice deep within my soul promised.

I chose to ignore it and continued to worry. Each time Don left, I begged God to watch out for him. The prayers did little to comfort my growing sense of panic.

Around this time, my second mystery *When Colette Died* was released. I left on a three-day promotional tour that took me to Albuquerque. I was scheduled to be on a mystery panel at a writer's conference and do four book signings at different bookstores in Albuquerque.

Friday, everything went smoothly. Then, Saturday morning at five, the jangling of the phone sent my blood pumping at great speeds.

"Mom, I'm on the way to the hospital. I was in a motorcycle accident, but I'm okay."

The only part I heard was motorcycle accident.

Motorcycle accident!

My fears had materialized. "How bad are you?"

"I'm okay."

My head spun. I couldn't think. I canceled the remaining autograph sessions and my husband and I rushed home. It normally takes about four hours to drive from Albuquerque to El Paso. These would be four long hours. Don had insisted that he was okay, but if so, why the hospital?

By the time we reached El Paso, Don had been admitted to the emergency room. He'd been there since six in the morning. He would not be released until after eight that night. As I visited him and talked to him, all the time I felt a strange detachment from my surroundings. I felt as if I was viewing the entire incident from the wrong end of a telescope.

The orderlies took Don to have some X-rays done. I grasped the opportunity to join Rich and Robert in the waiting room. I needed to know the details. Robert's narrative washed my soul with tranquility.

"It was a bit past midnight." Robert's eyes narrowed as he concentrated on the details. "Don called me from work. He'd forgotten to take the helmet and wanted me to bring it to him."

Wasn't this the same son who time after time had refused to wear the helmet? What had made him suddenly decide he needed it?

"I was tired. I was already asleep," Robert continued. "I didn't want to take it to him. I opened my mouth to say no, but then something made me change my mind."

"Something?"

"Yeah, something, like a feeling, a voice. Something."

Robert drove to Papa John's where Don worked and handed his brother the helmet. As they both touched it, somehow they knew. They looked at each other and each realized that the night still held secrets that would unfold.

"Be very careful, brother," Robert begged. "Be very careful."

"I know." Don nodded and Robert left.

Three hours later, Don finished doing the mandatory paper work that needed to be completed prior to closing. He locked up, mounted his motorcycle, and strapped on his helmet.

Three blocks later, Don watched the traffic light turn green. He started to cross the intersection. Off to his right, he saw a car approaching at great speed.

"He's not going to stop," Don told himself. "He's going to run the red light." But it was too late. Don had already committed himself to crossing the intersection.

Stay calm and think. Don't panic.

What could he do? His only option was to get out of the speeding car's way. He turned the throttle on the handlebar and sped away. The car missed him by inches, but the draft from the car caused Don to lose control of the bike.

As he tumbled down the street and his head hit the pavement several times, he could see the motorcycle fly above him. Don's fall came to a halt when he bumped into the curb. The motorcycle hit the same curb, flew over Don, and landed next to him. Had the curb not been there, the motorcycle would have landed on top of him.

But the curb was not the only thing that was there for him that fateful night. God had sent His angels to protect him. They had whispered to him and urged him to request the helmet.

They had also forced Robert to disregard how tired he felt and made sure that he'd deliver the requested item to his brother.

Every time I look at the damaged headgear, I notice one more scratch, one more dent. The eight-inch gash across the area protecting his chin means that the lower half of his face would have sustained severe damage. The gashes in the area intended to protect his forehead tell me his upper face would not have been spared either. Several dents and bumps visible throughout the back and sides of the helmet speak of brain damage. What would have happened if he hadn't been wearing the helmet?

The angels stood by him when the accident occurred. Something or someone prevented Don from panicking. He accelerated instead of slowing down, or worse, coming to a complete halt. The curb prevented the motorcycle from landing on top of him. Who had orchestrated all of these miracles?

I can clearly recall the anxiety eating at me like a carnivorous animal when I realized Don would purchase that motorcycle. I remember asking God who was going to take care of my son, and His promise comes to my mind, "I will." Yet, in spite of this, I nurtured the blaze of growing terror in my soul.

Although the motorcycle was completely ruined, Don walked away without a single broken bone. He was bruised, walked with a limp for several days, and will have permanent scars, but he was, as he had said, "Okay."

That day both Don and I learned something from the accident. I now realize that no matter how old Don gets or where he goes or what he does, I don't have to worry and wonder who is going to watch over him. He's got someone very powerful watching him.

He's got God's angels.

And I have peace in my heart.

Daniel in the Lions' Den

The Bible tells several stories about angels providing protection. One of the best known is about Daniel who petitioned God in prayer. This angered King Darius. He had decreed that he was the only one who can be petitioned.

Daniel needed to be punished for breaking the rules. The king ordered that Daniel be thrown into a den of hungry lions.

When King Darius went to Daniel the next day, he found that the lions had not eaten him. Daniel told the king that angels had come to seal the lions' mouths shut.

Miracle 8

The Bite

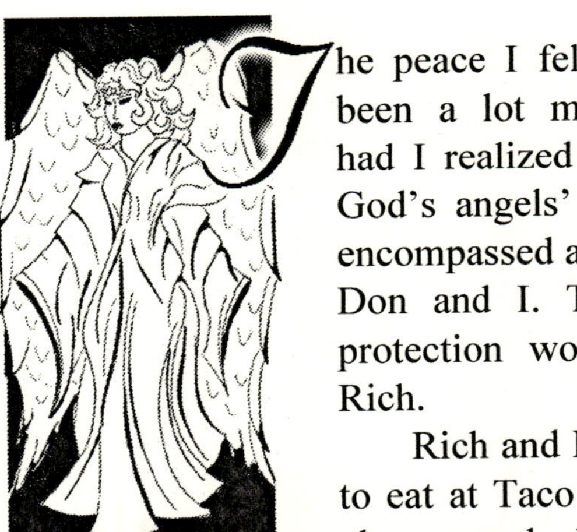

The peace I felt would have been a lot more profound had I realized the extent of God's angels' protection. It encompassed a lot more than Don and I. This time the protection would focus on Rich.

Rich and I had gone out to eat at Taco Bell. We had almost reached home when I realized that I, like a ding-a-ling, had left my purse behind at the fast food restaurant. Rich turned around and we headed back.

As we went around the block, we noticed that a woman and a group of children stood in a circle in the middle of the street. Then we saw the reason for the gathering: someone had run over their Rottweiler.

Rich pulled over and asked if he could help.

The woman looked up at him gratefully and said, “Yes, please. My kids don’t want to leave the dog alone. He’s very heavy and I can’t move him. If you can get him to the sidewalk, I can take care of the rest.”

Rich could see that the dog was in pain and that the street where the children congregated around the wounded animal was busy. He understood the mother’s concern. He bent down and gently scooped the dog in his arms.

The dog yelped and did the only thing he could to protect himself. He bit Rich. Blood gushed from Rich’s left hand and wrist. I asked Rich if he wanted me to drive him to the emergency room. He reassured me that he felt well enough to drive.

However, instead of heading for the emergency room, he stopped at Taco Bell. I ran in, found my purse just where I had left it, hanging on the same chair I had used during dinner. The purse’s contents were intact.

We then drove home where my husband applied first aid to the wounds. Since this was a Friday night, I spent my time calling various clinics to see which remained open.

All were closed.

The only choice we had left called for visiting the emergency room. We felt lucky to find one that wasn't so crowded and was willing to take Rich in right away.

The doctor cleaned out Rich's wounds, and, as a part of standard procedure, checked his blood pressure. The doctor found it to be excessively high and refused to release him until his blood pressure went down.

"Well, of course my blood pressure is going to be high," Rich said in his defense. "I've just been bitten by a dog. What do you expect?"

The doctor shook his head. "You don't understand." He raised his hand, palm facing downward, to shoulder height and said, "There's high blood pressure." He raised his hand the rest of the way and continued, "And then, there's your blood pressure."

The doctor gave Rich some nitroglycerin capsules, and we waited for the pressure to drop. An hour later the doctor returned to check Rich's pressure. Surely by now, he would be all right.

The doctor checked him and shook his head. "The medicine hasn't had any effect. Let's try another dose of nitroglycerin." He ordered Rich to remain flat on his back.

After another waiting period, the doctor returned to check on Rich again. Even though his blood pressure was still dangerously high, he allowed Rich to go home.

"Promise me that you'll visit your personal physician tomorrow," the doctor said. "Do you realize how lucky you are? If that dog hadn't bitten you. . ." He let the rest of the thought unspoken.

Rich promised to make an appointment with his doctor. When we returned home, there was a message on the answering machine. The dog had died, but the mother wanted to thank Rich for stopping to help. She wondered how he was doing.

Rich kept his word about visiting the doctor. Now, every day Rich takes his medicine to control the high blood pressure. As he does, we remember how "lucky" he was that I left my purse at Taco Bell and that a Rottweiler gave up his life to save Rich's.

First Cherubs

We've all seen drawings of baby angels, you know, those cute little cherubs, but have you ever wondered who the first cherub was? He comes from Greek or Roman mythology, and he's known as Cupid (Greek) or Eros (Roman). You'll recognize him as our Valentine symbol, for he is the god of love. This is one angel that hasn't changed since ancient times.

Miracle 9

A Ride with Destiny

I remember thanking God for sending that Rottweiler and then adding, "But next time, we could use something a little bit less dramatic."

I got my wish.

Rich and I were lazing at home when the phone rang. Don's girlfriend called to tell us that he had been hurt.

My heart did great aerobic leaps as I tried to figure out how I could learn about Don's condition. Since at that time he was a new recruit in the United States Air Force, there was no possible way for me to contact him except through the Red Cross and that, I assumed, would take several days.

Rich and I grabbed a handful of clothes and

headed for Wichita Falls, Texas, where Don was stationed at Sheppard Air Force Base. It was a bit past six on Friday, and we had just driven past the small town of Carlsbad, New Mexico.

When we learned that Don had been hurt, we rushed to his side. Here, he's getting ready to graduate from Boot Camp.

Feeling as anxious as I, Rich pushed the car to its limits. The speedometer needle fluctuated between seventy-five and eighty. We were a flying machine sailing smoothly down America's road.

Then Rich slowed down to seventy-five, then seventy, sixty-five. . .

"What's wrong?" I focused my attention on the declining speedometer. "Why are we slowing down?"

A frown formed on Rich's forehead. "I'm not doing it. In fact, I got my foot on the accelerator and I'm pushing it all the way down."

I could see that. I looked out the window. We weren't climbing any hills, but the speedometer needle had dropped to fifty-five.

Then we heard a large *thump,* followed by another, and still another.

Oh no, I thought. Car trouble.

Rich pulled off the side of the road and looked under the hood. Everything seemed normal. He checked the tires. They were fine. He got back in the car. "Let's keep going and see what happens," he said.

I said a small prayer and agreed.

The car started with no problem, but still it

would not accelerate like it was supposed to. As we drove down the freeway, we noticed that the *thump* we had picked up before had become a steady pattern.

"We're turning back." Rich made a U-turn and headed back toward Carlsbad.

I sighed and nodded. I knew we had no choice. "Do you think we'll be able to find a mechanic this late at night?" I looked at my watch. It was seven ten.

"Let's hope so." Rich pulled into the first gas station. He asked the attendant about the possibility of any mechanic shops still being open.

The man scratched his chin and said, "Nah. They'll all be closed by now." His eyes popped open as he looked across the street. "Hey, Mister, you're in luck. Seems like our mechanic is still working." He pointed to an open garage door two blocks down but still visible from the gasoline station.

We immediately headed that way.

The mechanic agreed to check the car. "Why don't you all go have dinner? By the time you get back, I'll have the problem fixed."

Rich and I walked to Pizza Hut and an hour later, we were back at the garage.

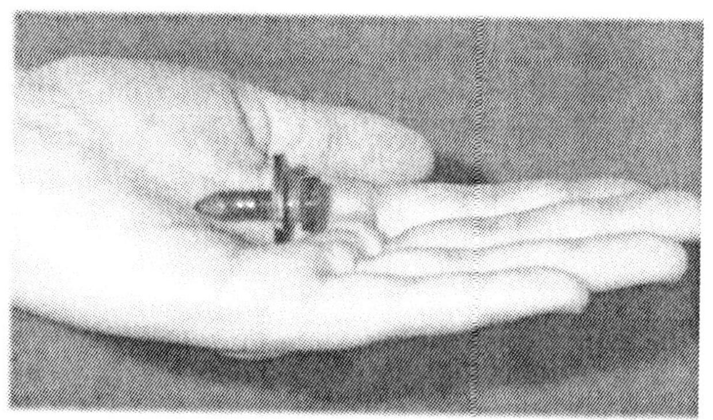

The mechanic removed this bolt and washer from the tire.

We both knew that it was too much to hope for, but Rich decided to ask the mechanic anyway. "Is the car ready?"

"Yep." The mechanic handed Rich a two-inch long bolt with a washer that measured an inch-and-a-half in diameter. "That's your culprit right there."

Rich looked at him, a question mark stamped on his face.

"I found the source of the noise. That was it." He pointed to the tire. "You had a flat. You hadn't lost any pressure yet, but if you'd continue to drive at high speeds, that tire would have surely blown. So I fixed your flat."

"That's good." Confusion remained evident in Rich's face. "What about the engine? What was wrong with it?"

"I checked everything and then I checked it again. There's absolutely nothing wrong with your engine. It purrs like a kitten."

"But it wouldn't let me accelerate."

The mechanic shrugged. "It does now."

"Then why couldn't I do it before?"

"Don't know. Nothing wrong with the engine. Like I said, you had a flat that would have blown if you'd been speeding."

Still feeling a bit confused, we thanked him, paid him, and drove off. The car accelerated just like it was supposed to. I looked at the car's antenna. A while back, I had attached an antenna angel to the radio antenna. I had no doubt in my mind, my angel had been there for us. For the rest of the time we drove that car, it never did that again.

As the mechanic said, there was no reason for the engine's failure to accelerate—except that if we had been speeding. . .

Angels and Hierarchy

In the fourth century, religious scholars not only labored over the writings of Paul, they also studied Ephesians 1:21 and Colossians 1:16. The scholars' end result consisted of creating a hierarchy of angels. Here then is the hierarchy of angels beginning with the most powerful and hallowed.

The First Hierarchy consists of Seraphim, Cherubim, and Thrones. The Second Hierarchy consists of Dominions, Principalities, and Powers. The Third Hierarchy consists of Virtues, Archangels, and Angels.

However, we have no way of knowing if

this is accurate or if the hierarchy truly exists. The hierarchy is merely man's way of ranking these heavenly creatures, something we feel compelled to do for nearly everything. Several other versions exist.

Miracle 10

Getting Us There

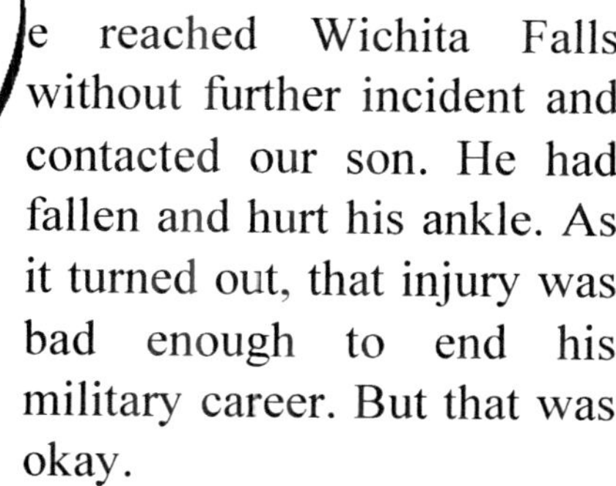

We reached Wichita Falls without further incident and contacted our son. He had fallen and hurt his ankle. As it turned out, that injury was bad enough to end his military career. But that was okay.

We can adjust, and while we're adjusting, we might as well enjoy ourselves so we decided to travel. Don and Robert were reaching adulthood, and as time marched on, my husband and I realized that our time to travel together as a family was coming to an end.

"So let's make this one a real nifty family vacation," I suggested.

We labored over the map and finally decided on Alaska. We would take the cruise and inside-passage tours. We all liked this idea, so we made the travel arrangements.

We planned to fly from El Paso to Salt Lake City, Utah, then to Seattle and then to Vancouver where we'd board the Princess cruise ship. That evening at six, our adventure would begin.

Or so we thought.

Our real adventure began way before we set foot on the cruise ship. It began at the airport in El Paso, Texas.

The Continental flight was scheduled to leave at seven in the morning. We reached the airport a bit before six. As we waited in line to check our luggage, our hearts filled with anticipation. We could hardly wait to get to Alaska, but for the moment, we had to wait.

We went to the waiting area, knowing full well that within minutes we'd be leaving for Utah. We heard the attendants call other flights, but not ours. We continued to wait. As the minutes ticked by, we exchanged worried glances with the other passengers also waiting to board the flight.

Ten minutes before the scheduled flight, a

Continental representative came out. "As you may have guessed, we're experiencing a minor mechanical problem, and the flight will be delayed. Right now, we expect to be airborne by seven thirty. If this creates a problem for you, please come see me."

Rich and I exchanged looks.

He gave a half-hearted shrug. "We have a three hour layover in Salt Lake City, we might as well just wait here."

I agreed.

We considered having breakfast but had less than half-an-hour to eat. We chose to wait. An hour later, we were still waiting. The attendant assured us that the plane would be ready in fifteen to twenty minutes. We had no choice but to continue to wait.

Nine o'clock came and went and it found us still stranded at the El Paso airport. Rich and I started to worry. Could we get to Utah in time to make our Seattle connection? We decided to talk to the attendant.

"We must board the ship prior to six. If we don't, it's going to sail without us."

"Oh, don't worry about that. We'll get you there in plenty of time." The attendant handed us a piece of paper. "Here's a voucher. You and your family can have breakfast on us."

We gratefully accepted the bribe. After all, none of us had eaten since yesterday. We headed for the airport's café. Its aroma gripped our stomachs and made us salivate. We placed our order and dreamed of the time when we would finally eat. Our eyes popped with delight as we saw the waitress approach our table with a tray filled with food.

On the opposite side of the room, we saw the Continental representative running toward us. She reached us before the food did.

Bummer.

"We found a flight for you." The Continental representative had obviously been running and fought to catch her breath and speak at the same time. "It's a Southwest flight bound for Los Angeles. From there you can take the Delta flight to Seattle. You'll only have ten minutes to make the transfer, but that's the only flight that will get you there on time. If you don't make that flight, you're not going to be sailing out tonight. Now, there's a small problem. The flight leaves in five minutes. Can you make it?"

We looked longingly at the food, jumped out of our chairs, and said, "Sure."

"Follow me." She led the way down to the waiting airline. "This was so sudden that we didn't even have a chance to transfer your luggage. It'll catch up with you in two to three days."

Double bummer.

We boarded the Southwest plane, took off into the sky, eagerly ate our peanuts, and washed them down with the soda. When the stewardess picked up the empty cans and trash, Rich explained our dilemma about having to catch the Delta flight scheduled to take off ten minutes after we were to land. "What's the best way to go?" he asked.

Her eyebrows arched in surprise. "Didn't anybody at Continental bother to explain to you about the Los Angeles terminal?"

Minor detail. Rich and I exchanged glances. We do that a lot.

"Not really," he said.

"We're on opposite ends of the terminal," she said.

Oh, oh. We were in trouble.

"Tell you what," the Southwest stewardess said. "Let me tell the pilot. He'll contact the Delta authorities, tell them we're already in flight, and request that they hold the flight for you and your family."

We thanked her and she headed for the cockpit.

She returned a few minutes later. From the look on her face, we knew she didn't have good news. "No deal." She looked down at the floor as though it had been her fault. "Best I can do for you is move you up to the front, right before we land. This way you can be the first ones out."

She did more than that. Not only were we the first ones out, a Southwest representative waited for us as soon as we stepped out. "Can you run?" she asked.

We said, "Yes," and we ran after her as she led us to a parked car, waiting with its doors open. We had all barely jumped in when the driver took off and leapfrogged through traffic.

While he drove, he gave us instructions about how to get to the proper Delta gate. "I'd advise you to choose one of you to run ahead of the others. Then that person can hold the flight for the other three."

Everybody looked at me.

Lucky me.

The car barely rolled to a stop when I jumped out and ran down the corridors as instructed. I reached the area, and between breaths, I told the Delta employee I was here for the Seattle flight.

She pointed behind her, up toward the sky. "See that plane?"

A sinking feeling settled in my heart. I nodded.

"That's the one you just missed."

Triple bummer. Now what?

We returned to the Continental area since they were the ones responsible for this mess. We explained to the Continental representative our dilemma. "We have to be on the ship at six when it sails."

"No problem," she said. "We'll simply put you on the next flight." She pounded on the computer keys and retrieved some information. She smiled awkwardly at us. "Seems the earliest we can get you there is seven o'clock."

"That won't do," I said. "The ship sails at six."

She pounded some more on her computer. She retrieved additional information—or maybe it was the same thing all over again. She called her supervisor and explained what was going on.

He called his supervisor.

"Why don't you call the cruise line and see if they can delay departure until the Haydens get there?"

Okay. Here we go again.

"No problem," the cruise lines people said. "We can wait that one hour if the Haydens are willing to pay the extra one hour docking fee."

"How much is it?" I asked.

They told me.

I almost fainted.

I looked at the Continental representatives. "Your company's the one that originally messed up. Your company should pay the docking fee."

They nearly fainted.

Now all three Continental representatives returned to the keyboard, pounded on the keys, and conferred in soft voices. "We can fly you to the first port-of-call and you can join the cruise there," one of the supervisors suggested.

That would mean we'd lose the first two days of sailing. We'd also miss cruising past the Inside Passage, one of the most beautiful sights in the Alaska cruise. We were all looking forward to seeing and photographing the Inside Passage.

I shook my head. "We paid a lot of money for a seven-day cruise. If we take you up on your offer, our cruise will be cut to five days."

The supervisor frowned and pounded some more keys.

The phone rang. "Hello?" he snarled. As he listened, his features softened. "Just a minute. Let me check." He dashed back to the computer and smiled. "They'll be there."

He hung up. "That was the Princess Cruise line wanting to know if the Haydens are still here." He paused for effect. "Seems like some folks, who are going to take the same cruise you folks are, were loaded into a bus and were being taken to the airport. The bus had a flat tire, and they missed their flight. The cruise line has no choice but to wait for those folks because it's their own bus line. If we can connect you to the folks in Sacramento, then they can get you to the ship in time." He smiled. "And that we can do."

We hooked up with the folks from Sacramento, and we went on to have a wonderful time on our last family cruise.

And the only reason we were able to make the cruise was because a bus in Sacramento had a flat tire just when we needed one.

Quite a coincidence, huh?

While in Alaska, the four of us,
Robert, Don, Rich and I,
took a helicopter ride that landed on a glacier.

Archangel Michael

The Bible describes angel deeds in various places. One of the best-known stories centers on the Archangel Michael. Jude 1:9 and Revelation 12:7-9 tells of his conflict with Satan. Daniel 6:22 relates that God sent Michael to Daniel to tell him that God would protect him from the

Persians.

Miracle 11

The Mechanical Angel

Thinking back, I could see that several of our personal miracles have centered on something mechanical: a car that won't accelerate; a car that won't start; a bus with a flat tire. This causes me to wonder, does my Guardian Angel enjoy fidgeting with mechanical things? I toyed with the thought when once again, we experienced another mechanical miracle.

Even before my mystery novels were released, Rich and I, both being teachers, spent our summers traveling. We felt that traveling served as a fun educational experience for our sons.

Then, when *Who's Susan?* came out, the

reason for traveling doubled. Promoting books means visiting the various bookstores, doing autograph sessions, speaking in libraries, schools, organizations, or clubs. In addition, I do television interviews and radio shows.

To facilitate matters, we bought a motor home and it is just that, our home away from home. Once we reach our travel destination, we park the camper and use our Honda CRV, which we tow, to drive to the desired locations, usually within a two hundred-mile radius.

After the release of my third mystery, *Where Secrets Lie*, we retired and our traveling summers extended to an entire year. On this one particular day, we were heading toward Plano, Texas, for the Cluefest Mystery Convention. We hadn't yet reached Abilene when a man driving a red, jeep Cherokee pulled in front of us.

Rich slammed on the brakes to avoid hitting him. The man slowed down even more, rolled down his window, and signaled for us to pull over. Rich felt leery, but did so anyway.

The man stepped out of his car and approached us. "Smoke is coming out of your tow vehicle's engine."

Rich thanked him for telling us and ran

toward the car. He lifted the hood and a plume of gray smoke bellowed out.

Not knowing what to do, we waited for over half-an-hour for the engine to cool and stop smoking. Then we continued to tow it at a much lower speed. Abilene lay thirty miles ahead. I sat on top of the bed in the motor home, keeping a watchful eye on the Honda's engine. Those thirty miles were very long miles.

On the outskirts of Abilene, we stopped at the Flying-J Truck Stop. The attendants there told us they had three mechanics on call twenty-four hours a day.

The first mechanic was unreachable.

The other two said they could fix eighteen-wheelers, but not car engines. They did refer us to a shop that remained opened twenty-four hours a day, and luckily was just two blocks away. We could easily walk that distance.

When we reached this twenty-four hour shop, we let out a sigh of relief.

We shouldn't have.

The twenty-four hour shop was closed.

Fortunately, the sign in front of the shop listed an emergency number.

I zipped out my cell phone and punched in the numbers.

No answer.

Across the street, a gas station beckoned. The attendants told us that they were strictly a gas station with no mechanical repair facilities. "But if you look kitty-corner from us, you'll see a shop that specializes in eighteen-wheelers."

Oh, sigh.

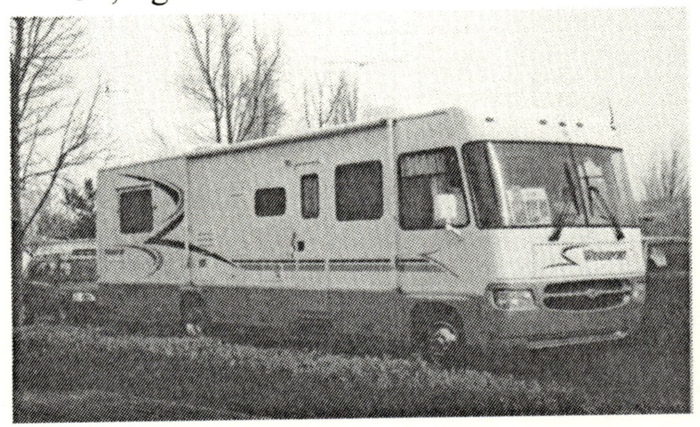

Here's our motorhome towing our Honda CRV.

We went to it anyway.

The place was officially closed, but three mechanics hung around, shooting the bull. They all admitted that they didn't know much about car engines, but were willing to look at it anyway.

We walked back to the Flying-J where we

had left the camper and the car. Rich drove the motor home, and I drove the car to the mechanic's shop.

None of the three mechanics could find anything wrong with the engine. The youngest of the mechanics frowned. "It seems to me that your car is in perfect working condition. I suggest that you tow the Honda at a slow speed all the way to Plano. They have a Honda dealership there."

The other two agreed.

We did just that.

But first we towed it past Plano to Melissa where we had our campground reservations. While Rich unhooked the jeep, I got dressed for the conference.

Rich drove me back to Plano, dropped me off at the hotel conference site, then drove to the Honda dealership.

Rich explained to the mechanic what had happened.

He shook his head in disbelief. "You said you drove it here?"

Rich nodded.

"That's impossible. Cars that smoke like that means the transmission is shot. That car should be undriveable."

After checking the car, the mechanics found nothing wrong. They emptied all the fluids and replaced them, just in case. The total bill was under two hundred dollars, not the several thousand we expected for a new transmission.

Just to be on the safe side, the head mechanic decided to call the Honda headquarters.

The person on the other end echoed everyone's amazement. "What? You said he drove the car in? That's impossible. You mean he towed it in, right?"

No, Rich had driven it in, and now, almost a year later, we're still driving the Honda.

We never did find the reason for the delay. But we do wonder what would have happened if we had continued to drive with the engine smoking.

We were "lucky" that a man driving a red, jeep Cherokee just happened to be passing us at the moment our engine decided to start smoking.

We were "lucky" that he happened to spot the smoke. We were lucky that he decided to tell us.

We were "lucky". . .

Angels and Numbers

How many times have you heard, "What's your lucky number ?"

How many times have you heard "seven" as the answer?

The number seven is mentioned in the Bible, as in the seven deadly sins, but also as the number of Angels of Revelation. Each carries his vial of the seven last plagues.

Miracle 12

The Healing

Beauty surrounds us: the roaring of the majestic sea, the gallant effort of a single flower blooming in the desert, or the trees gently swaying in the forest. I love it all.

I find that the best way to absorb nature's beauty is to hike the many trails our national parks offer. Although Rich and I are not professional hikers, we have become at least adequate at hiking—that is, until Rich's knee started giving him problems.

Still, we didn't let that stop us. We continued to hike, often selecting the easier trails that call for almost no climbing. However, by the time we finished with our hike, I could see the pain in Rich's face.

I considered not doing any more hikes, and when my writing took us back to the San Antonio/Austin area, I felt delighted. Both Rich and I love this part of Texas, and the activities there do not involve hiking.

Since we have been to either San Antonio or Austin at least ten to fifteen times before, we both feel that we know all of the tourist places. Travel brochures do not attract our attention.

That's why it came as a shock to me when Rich headed straight for the travel brochures displayed at the motel in San Antonio. After glancing at the rack, Rich picked up a brochure. "Look. I've found a new place to visit. A Russian Orthodox Monastery six miles southwest of Blanco. That's not too far from here." He handed me the brochure.

I looked at it and saw that its cover displayed an Icon of Virgin Mary. According to the brochure, the Icon wept continuously from May until October 1985, and continues to weep intermittently even to this day.

That piqued our interest.

The next day, we drove to the monastery. We found a peaceful place where the monks live a simple life. The monks invited us to attend an upcoming service, and then afterward, they would anoint each one of us with tears from the icon. The monks informed us that many people have experienced miracles after the anointment.

We accepted their invitation and attended. Shortly after the anointment, we left the monastery, feeling peaceful and calm, but not really changed.

A few days later, Rich and I decided to go hiking, and as usual, we knew Rich's knee would act up. We took what we thought would be an easy trail, but as it turned out, certain areas involved steep climbing.

More than two hours later, we returned to our car. Rich's hand froze on the ignition key.

I looked at him. Amazement covered his face.

"My knee didn't act up."

I stared at him. We had been so busy climbing, we hadn't noticed that his knee hadn't bothered him.

The next day we decided to do a different hike. This time, we purposely chose one listed as being a bit strenuous. As before, Rich's knee did not cause him any problems. Nor did it bother him the time after that or the one after that or. . .

We've often wondered if another miracle could be attributed to the Icon of Virgin Mary. What we do know is that something compelled Rich to look at the brochures.

That one single action—an action he seldom takes—healed his knee problem.

What—who—had urged him to seek the brochures?

Queen of Angels

Who is the Queen of Angels, or Our Lady of the Angels, or Mother of Angels? She is Mary, mother of Christ. Catholics believe that she loves the angels and considers them her own children. Many who have seen her also claim to have seen angels accompanying her.

Miracle 13

A Miracle in the Making

For as long as I can remember, grottos—shrines usually built inside of caves—have captivated my interest. I had always thought that if I ever made a substantial amount of money from writing, I'd like to build a grotto.

I'd call it The Garden of Peace. It would not only be a beautiful place filled with flowers and hopefully a stream, but it would also be a peaceful, quiet area where people could meditate, refresh themselves, and leave the gardens filled with hope, love, and faith.

What size, where, how, when—I had never

considered these details. All I know is that for each book I sell, I set aside a percentage to go toward building The Garden of Peace.

The name, by the way, is not my original idea. A fan from Las Cruces, New Mexico, came up with the name. I met her during one of my autograph sessions. We began talking and somehow we ended up discussing my dream.

Much to my surprise, she too has similar expectations. She suggested that I contact her when I'm ready to start building. She knows a lot about plants and will be able to help design the garden.

A rush of excitement ran through me. Plants and I have never gotten along. They see me coming and they die. (The exception is weeds. Those refuse to die. Remember?)

Looking back, I think that meeting my new friend is another one of those "coincidences." What had led her to come to the bookstore at the moment I was doing a signing? What had prompted me to tell her about my dream to build this garden? Finally, and most importantly, am I really supposed to build this garden?

Exquisite woodcarvings adorn the trail in Portland's grotto.

The coincidences run deeper than this. As I mentioned before, I have always been fascinated with grottos. Rich will drive out of the way if he knows of one in the vicinity.

It is, of course, a special delight when we find one right on our scheduled path. It happened on our recent Portland, Oregon, trip. When my second mystery novel *When Colette Died* was released, part of my promotional tour called for some signings in Portland and its surrounding area.

While waiting for the weekend to arrive, we decided to visit the grotto in Portland. As we approached the entrance, I noticed the man with his back to us. He seemed deep in thought as he stood in front of one of the many religious statues.

We were still behind him when he abruptly turned toward us, giving me the impression that he had been expecting us. "Hello." His smile reached all the way to his eyes. "Have you been here before?"

What I wanted to ask him was how he knew we were there. Instead, I answered his question. "No, we haven't."

"Then let me give you the tour."

He led us up the trail and stopped beside each statue. He explained the significance behind the figures. We continued our stroll down the trail and stopped to listen to the stream running through the lush, green gardens. We marveled at the wide variety of colors that the flowers offered.

We felt awed by the beautiful woodcarvings depicting scenes from Jesus's life. We stopped at the end of the trail at the life-size replica of Michelangelo's famous *Pietá*. Located inside of a cave, the reproduction of the artist's work is surrounded with green ferns. Two angels, holding torches, guard the entrance. At the foot of each angel, seven lit candles illuminate the way.

Throughout our tour, our guide told us a bit about himself. He said that he loves the grotto and spends a lot of time there.

As we wandered through the well-kept gardens, I noticed we were the only ones with a personal guide. Because he took it upon himself to show us around, he greatly enhanced our experience of the grotto. We learned things that we wouldn't have known otherwise.

But the fact that he singled us out to give us the tour is not the amazing part of my grotto experience. Often, our guide would say things that made me feel as though he had an insight into my life. It was never a specific fact, but more like a general statement that became a whisper in the wind.

As we approached yet another statue, our guide looked at me. "Mothers who have problems with their children come here to pray." He pointed to the statue. "This is the Virgin Mary's Mother, St. Ann, the Mother of All Mothers. You should give her a try."

A life-size reproduction of Michelangelo's Pietá greets visitors in this grotto in Portland, Oregon.

His words hit me like a rock. At that time, my life was wrapped around my son's many problems. I wondered if this was the kind of statement our self-appointed tour guide made to everyone. Or was it said for my benefit?

At another time he said, "People are talkers. Few are doers." Then he looked straight at Rich and opened his arms, signifying the area. "Why don't you build a grotto like this?"

Another question he asks everyone?

I'm scheduled to return to Portland very soon. I plan to visit the grotto again. Maybe then I'll see if I'm reading too much into this.

Or maybe I'll find some answers.

We'll see.

Angels as Providers of Courage

When we have an especially hard task to perform, it seems natural that we raise our voices and ask for courage to finish whatever task we've been assigned.

Such was the case with Jesus. When Jesus went to pray at the Garden of Gethsemane, an angel appeared to Him. The angel had come to provide Jesus with courage.

Miracle 14

A Bit of Heaven

Like most newlywed couples, Rich and I dreamed about our future together. We decided we would retire at an early age so we could enjoy ourselves. We would travel and get to know the world. Trying different and new things would allow us to taste life at its fullest.

Then the magical date arrived: May 25, 2001. Both Rich and I turned in our keys and walked out of our classrooms after teaching for over twenty-five years. We felt eager and confident as we began the new phase of our lives.

Years before our retirement date, Rich and I spent a vast amount of time considering where we'd like to live after we retired. Our dreams ran along the same lines. We'd buy a couple of acres where the silence of night would shout at us. The sky would no longer conceal its millions of twinkling stars, and the gurgling stream would lullaby us to sleep.

During the day we'd kayak on our pond as we watched the ducks frolic, or we'd rest under the shade of the large trees on our land, and when there was work to do, we'd get a tractor to help us. Rich would drive it, and I'd get rides in its trailer. Now that's hard work, huh?

Then reality hit.

Being an author involves a lot of traveling. If we're gone for a month or more, who would watch our place? We'd basically have no neighbors, and those we did have, we probably wouldn't know.

So okay, a house on acreage wouldn't work. Bummer.

Time to move on to Plan Two. A snowbird community, very similar to the one where our younger son, Robert, is now living in Tucson, would be ideal. No matter how long we were gone, our place would be safe.

Then came the glitch. When our sons went away to school, we promised them we'd watch their dogs. Much to our dismay, Don and Robert had become the proud owners of two large dogs, so now we have these big dogs to love and care for.

Our search for snowbird communities revealed that most places restrict the number of pets. One small dog is the maximum. We love our dogs (even though they are not technically ours) and wouldn't dream of giving them up.

Enter Plan Three. We could host a campground. Depending on which one we chose to host, we could have a stream, and if we got lucky, we'd also have a pond or lake in which we could kayak. The stars would be there for us at night, and best of all, our doggies would be with us. We'd live in our motor home and occasionally return to our permanent home in El Paso.

Plan Three enticed us.

The only question that now remained was where did this magical campground exist? Since we're constantly traveling to the Austin/San Antonio area, that was the most logical place to search. We fell in love with the Texas Hill Country.

We found a campground and spent a couple of days there. The place turned out to be ideal.

We could go tubing on the river and watch the wildlife that visited the campgrounds daily.

The only thing we could find wrong with the area was that the dogs would always have to be chained. This was a bummer, of course, but no matter where we'd host, the dogs would always have to be on a leash.

We talked to the hosts and became great friends with them. We picked up the proper application forms. We knew exactly where we would host our first campground.

As retirement neared, we eagerly marked the days until we could temporarily live in the Texas Hill Country.

After we retired, but prior to the time we could host, we found ourselves making several trips to Arizona simply because our sons live there.

Once, on our way home from Phoenix, we saw the sign for the cutoff to Roper Lake State Park. We weren't in a hurry to get home, so we decided to pull in and see what Roper Lake was all about.

That's when we found our bit of heaven.

We talked to some of the hosts and to the head ranger. They made us feel welcome and invited us to host at Roper Lake. They showed us where we would park our motor home.

The area is not actually in Roper Lake, but at Dankworth Ponds, three miles away from the lake. Our motor home would be parked in what the rangers refer to as the compound, a large enclosed area. We wouldn't have to chain the dogs after all. Instead, they would have plenty of space to run and explore.

A small creek, which comes from a natural hot springs, runs through the area. Outside the compound, there's a pond, and three miles away, a lake where we can swim or kayak. There are plenty of nature trails and natural hot tubs.

Large shade trees provide comfort and beauty. At night, millions of stars twinkle our welcome.

The park's location is also ideal. It's only two hours away from Tucson (where Robert lives,) three hours away from Phoenix (where Don lives,) and four hours away from El Paso (our home.)

As I write this, I'm sitting under the shade of a large tree, listening to the gurgling sounds of the stream. I look around the compound and marvel at the idea of how we found this place.

We never even considered hosting in

Arizona. It was always going to be in our home state of Texas. Yet, something—someone?—led us to this bit of heaven.

After working on the trail at Dankworth Ponds in Arizona, I would hop on the trailer and get a ride back to our motorhome.

And oh, remember I mentioned the tractor? We have the use of one. We use it to haul off the limbs of trees we prune and for other work-related jobs. But when we bring it back to the compound, I always get to ride in its empty trailer.

Nature formed this ice angel when a hose burst.

One night the temperatures dipped into the freezing digits. While we slept, one of the hoses outside broke and water squirted out. It immediately froze, and the formation of frozen arches was a sight to behold.

But more awe inspiring than those arches was the formation leading to those icy lines. The water had formed itself into the shape of an angel.

I knew then that it must have been an angel who led us to this bit of heaven.

Folk Sayings

Even folklore has contributed to the popularity of angels. As the saying goes, "Nothing is hidden from the angels."

Afterthought

My promotional tours for my mysteries are, if anything, time consuming. A typical promotional tour would begin the day after the school year ends. Rich and I, both being teachers, always used the summers to promote the books. We'd spend the entire summer on the road and arrive home only the day before we were scheduled to return to work.

As my writing career developed, I found that I could no longer travel just during the summers. In May 2001, Rich and I retired after teaching for twenty-six years. Since then, we have been on the road more than we've been home.

Almost every weekend since retirement in May 2001, we have visited a different city, a different state, signing books, doing television interviews, speaking to special interest groups, or attending conventions.

Our 2001 summer plan called for us to return home on July 3rd. We would unpack, repack, unwind, rewind and head out three days later. During those three days that we were home, my oldest son got so congested that he almost stopped breathing. His girlfriend and I rushed him to the emergency room. He received proper treatment and was released from the hospital several hours later.

The little time I had left, I devoted to catching up with my e-mail. I filled in my friends and family on what had happened during my tours and, of course, I told them about Don. One of the answers I received struck close to home.

Susan Streib, my good Internet buddy from West Virginia, wrote, “I know how far and how often you travel. Yet you just happened to be home at the exact moment that you were needed. I find this to be quite a coincidence.”

Ahh. A coincidence.

Is it because I’m such a lucky gal?

I don’t think so. I don’t feel luckier than most.

What I am is a bit more perceptive. I realize that miracles can and do surround us. I feel very grateful for each and every one, not just those I mentioned here, but all the others whether I recognize them or not.

I sincerely hope that now that you have read bits and pieces of the miraculous events in my life, you will want to reflect on those in your own. In your own way, in your own time, you'll be able to feel the angels' invisible powers, listen to their silent voices, and grasp some new knowledge. You'll find that if you open yourself to miracles, they are yours for the asking. For miracles will abound *When Angels Touch You.*

A Common Word

Angels are so popular that we seem to surround ourselves with them. If we're hungry, we feast on angel hair pasta and for dessert, there's always angel food cake. While eating, we put on the CD and listen to our favorite artist who "sings like an angel."

Afterward, we glance at the pictures we took of our recent trip to Venezuela. We're particularly fascinated by the one of Angel Falls, the longest, uninterrupted waterfall in the world. Then there's the pictures of us scuba diving among the school of angelfish.

Now that we're ready for bed, we lock the door, for this is Los Angeles. We wonder if there are any “angels of mercy” in this City of Angels. And of course, we check on our little one who is “sleeping like an angel.”

Today, we’re very proud of him. He “behaved like an angel” all day long, and we wonder if he’ll grow up to be a Hell’s Angel or a Blue Angel.

Part II:

Angels Around Us

Dear Readers,

As a writer, one of the questions people most often ask me is, "So what are you working on now?" When I told people about my angel/miracle project, I was surprised to hear how many of them have experienced equally miraculous incidents.

Most of these people wanted for me to tell you their stories. I promised them I would. Consequently, I have begun with Part II of the angel series. However, unlike *When Angels Touch You,* the next book will be about you.

If you have a story that you'd like to share about a miracle or an angel experience in your life, and you'd like for me to include it in *Angels Around Us*, please send it to me. Remember to be as specific as you can. Let me know how I can reach you in case I have any questions.

Please send your story and your comments to me at lchayden@lycos.com. For the subject, please type Angel Story, Miracle Story, or Miracle/Angel Comments.

The following true narratives are examples of the type of stories I am looking for.

I can hardly wait to hear about your wonderful experiences.

May the angels surround you,
L. C. Hayden

Angels as Guides

It seems that one of the angels' favorite ways to help mankind is by allowing us humans to be there for one another. Unfortunately, we're not always aware of someone else's needs. Sometimes, we're too wrapped up in our own desires and problems. At other times, we have no way of knowing that our loved ones or friends are reaching out for us. That's when the angels enter.

The Right Turn

Steve and Joan's story from Georgetown, Texas

Excitement filled the air. Steve, Joan, and their three kids had packed up the camper and headed toward South Padre Island State Park where they would meet some friends. They planned to spend the long weekend together.

As with most married couples, Steve and Joan took turns driving. At this particular moment, it was Joan's turn to drive. She followed the road signs and happily drove along the unfamiliar route.

About ten miles down the road, Steve woke up and looked around. An inquisitive frown formed on his face. He didn't recognize any of the landmarks Joan passed. "Where are we?"

"I just followed the road you told me to."

Steve caught sight of a road sign then looked at the map.

"Are we going the right way?" Joan asked.

Steve shook his head. "Nope, you took a wrong turn a few miles back. We're heading for Kingsville."

"I don't remember planning to go through Kingsville," Joan said as she maneuvered the truck and camper around a curve.

"Well, we're not too far off course. Looks like you followed the business route instead of staying on the main highway. Let's go into town and grab a drink and change drivers."

As they approached the town, Joan spotted a fast food restaurant up ahead. "Look, there's a McDonald's."

"That's a good place to pull in. You get us drinks and we'll stretch our legs."

When Joan entered the McDonald's, she

bumped into and nearly knocked over a young boy. When she took a second look she recognized him as being the son of the people they were meeting.

"What are you doing here? Where's your Mom and Dad?"

He looked up at her. "We were on the way down to meet you guys but we were in an accident. They took us all to the hospital and treated us but they admitted Mom."

"So who are you here with?" Joan looked around and spotted the boy's uncle who had come from out of town to help out in this situation.

Joan looked out the window toward the sky. What. . .or who had made her take the wrong turn down the road? Why had she chosen to stop at this particular McDonald's instead of any of the other places?

Perhaps an angel had whispered in her ear that her friends needed help and led her and Steve to the right place.

Gabriel

One of the many functions of angels is to serve as guides. The archangel Gabriel served as Muhammad's guide through the seven Islamic heavens. Those of the Islamic religion believe that if they are true believers, then two angels will serve them. One angel will hover over their left shoulder and keep a record of all the evil that they do. The angel hovering over their right will record the good deeds.

Providers of Comfort

Although no one can predict when and where an angel will appear, many people relate stories about angels helping them in their time of greatest need. Often, when we feel distraught, lonely, or hopeless, an angel, sometimes takes the form of a friendly stranger and reaches out.

It is then no wonder that when we mourn the death of a loved one, many stories relating to angels blossom. Often, the angels do not appear as the winged creatures we associate with the word angel, but instead are someone we know or love. Sometimes it may even be the person we are mourning…

Comfort from the Other Side

Eddy's Story from Ladonia, Texas

The first time Eddy's father called him, Eddy should have known something was wrong. But his dad insisted everything was okay.

"I'm taking Mama to the hospital, but don't

worry. She's okay. There's no use you driving two hours over here for nothing."

The second time the phone rang, Eddy immediately picked it up.

"Son, we're here in the hospital. Mama is okay so don't worry."

If his mother were really all right just like Dad claimed, why had he called to tell him basically the same thing? Wanting desperately to know exactly what was going on, he asked if his younger sister Sherri was with him.

"She's right here."

"Let me speak to her."

Her news stunned him. "Mama's on life support right now. She's swallowed her tongue, and they're going to do a brain scan to see if there's any brain activity left."

All the energy drained out of Eddy. Just a week ago, the last time he'd spoken to his mom, they'd had a serious fight. And now, she lay dying. How will she ever know he loved her and was sorry he had gotten angry with her? If only he could talk to her, just one more time, he'd let her know how sorry he was.

Although by now, it was past midnight, Eddy and his wife Cathy packed up their two children and Eddy settled back for the long drive.

The further he drove, the more the questions flooded his brain. *Will Mama be okay? Will I be able to talk to her? Will she ever know I really am sorry?*

Eddy knew that his last conversation with his mother would haunt him for the rest of his life. If only he could talk to her just one more time, maybe he could make it right.

He continued to drive, his mind focused on his desire to make peace with his mom. *If only God would send an angel right now. I need one so much.*

That's when he saw his mom.

Eddy felt vaguely aware that he was driving, but somehow, in front of him, he could clearly see his mom.

"I'm sorry I got mad at you. Are you okay? Dad said—Sherri said. . .What's wrong? What's going on?"

While driving, Eddy talked to his mom. He knew he should pull over so he could devote all of his attention to the conversation. "I'm going to pull over so we can talk."

She smiled at him. "I won't let anything happen to you. Don't worry about me. I'm dead and my body is at the hospital, but I'm here.

I'm happy and okay. I'm trying to talk to Sherri, but she won't listen to me. I only have a short time and I'm counting on you. It's very important to me. You have to make her listen."

Behind her stood a man Eddy vaguely recognized. He leaned down and said, "Come on, Sis. It's time to go. There's someone you need to meet."

That's when Eddy recognized him as Uncle Howell, his mom's only brother. Eddy looked past them and saw another man heading toward them.

Eddy's mom turned toward Eddy. "Goodbye, Son. Remember, I'm happy. Make Sherri listen to me."

Eddy watched as his mom and her brother gave their attention to the man who by now had reached them. Uncle Howell introduced him as their father. Eddy realized that his mom had not recognized her own father because she had been very young when her father passed away. They hugged and the three disappeared.

Eddy's attention returned to his driving. He had driven approximately fifteen miles, but had no recollection of having driven the distance. He knew his mom was dead, but he had peace in his heart. He knew she had forgiven him for getting angry. He could accept her death.

When Eddy and his family reached the hospital, he found Sherri. "Mama wants to talk to you. You need to listen." Sherri felt too heartbroken to make any sense of what her brother was telling her.

Again, Eddy tried. "Listen to her, Sherri."

Eventually, Sherri gave in. She looked out the window and a glazed look covered her eyes.

Eddy knew she was talking to Mama.

"She told me what dress she wants to be buried in, and she's concerned about Diane and Dan."

Diane and Dan, Eddy's other sister and brother, took their mother's death extra hard. Both Eddy and Sherri reached out to them. "Mama is happy. She wants you to know that."

Although Diana, Eddy, Dan, and Sherri grieved for their mother's death, all four felt comfort in the knowledge that one day they will be reunited. They knew that their mama was happy.

The peace they felt came directly from an angel—an angel they call Mama.

Jesus, Angels and Temptation

Since ages untold, angels have provided comfort and guidance. Knowing this, Satan dared Jesus to throw himself down from where historian Josephus claims to be a 450 feet drop in the Kedron Valley. Surely, angels would be there to catch him.

Jesus spurned Satan's attempts to tempt Him, and the angels came to look after Him.

Just as the angels ministered to Jesus, call upon them to help you in your need. They will pleasantly surprise you with their solace and comfort. They're just waiting for you to ask.

About the Author

L. C. Hayden has penned three mystery novels, *Where Secrets Lie*, *When Colette Died*, and *Who's Susan? When Angels Touch You* is the author's first nonfiction work. She has sold over 400 pieces to newspapers and magazines.

Hayden, a retired teacher, calls El Paso, Texas, her home, although she and her husband spend most of their time on the road in their motor home, promoting books, doing workshops, or speaking at schools and other organizations.

Hayden holds a Master's Degree in Creative Writing from the University of Texas at El Paso. Besides writing, Hayden enjoys drawing, reading, traveling, and scuba diving. She is a member of Sisters in Crime, Mystery Writers of America, Southwest Writers, and DL, and online mystery discussion group.

Contact the Author

L.C. Hayden invites you to visit her website at lchayden.freeservers.com. You can also contact her via email through her site.

You may email L. C. Hayden at
lchayden@lycos.com

She loves to hear from her readers.

L.C. Hayden's Mysteries

Where Secrets Lie
ISBN 1-929976-06-2 ($14.95)
(Hollywood legend Annie Francis has optioned this book for a movie.)

At her mother's deathbed, Lisa learns a horrible truth: at birth she was subject of an illegal adoption. Overwhelmed by the revelation, Lisa becomes obsessed with finding her biological parents. Her search takes her into the world of one of the wealthiest and most powerful men in America, James Johnson. But Johnson has a diabolical secret, which, if discovered, will destroy him. Lisa, unaware of this, continues to dig *Where Secrets Lie* and each step brings her closer to learning the secrets…and to danger.

Where Secrets Lie is an absorbing suspense novel, filled with red herrings that will have you dashing down many wrong turns in your efforts to solve the puzzle. Hayden brings such depth to her characters that you sometimes forget they aren't real. This is a good old-fashioned heroine in danger suspense novel that will keep you on the edge of your seat until the very last page.

Kathy Thomason
The Butler County Post
The Amplifier

When Colette Died
ISBN 0-9666366-6-X ($14.95)
(An Oprah-On Line Reading Selection)

Five years after the murder of Las Vegas singing superstar, Colette, Debbie Gunther is hired to impersonate the fallen star. Her dream job turns into a nightmare, when on her first day at the Crystal Palace Casino, she receives a threatening note. Then everything that had happened to Colette starts happening to her. She turns to Dan Springer. Together, they work to find the killer, for they know that if Debbie is to survive, they must discover what happened on the day *When Colette Died*.

The strongest point of Hayden's novel is the ability to create a truly readable story. By interweaving false leads with fascinating side plots, the author keeps her readers guessing until the very last page.

Myrna Zanetell
El Paso Scene

Who's Susan?
ISBN 0-9666366-1-9($9.95)
(A Barnes & Noble Top Ten Best Seller)

The first eighteen years of Susan Haynes's life are a complete blank. Finding her past is not a priority until she goes to the daycare center to pick up her four-year old son Timmy.

The center insists that Susan has already picked him up, but Susan knows better even though everyone doubts her. Susan is then forced to search alone for her son while the world around her crumbles as her past and present intersect to reveal a shocking truth. Sadly, Susan realizes that if she is to save her son's life, she must first answer the question: *Who's Susan?*

Here's one hot mystery story with a child in jeopardy, amnesia, a chase in the Southwestern desert. . . It's a novel with real people in real trouble. . . Highly recommended.

New Mystery Magazine

Coming Soon from L.C. Hayden

What Others Know
—A Harry Bronson Mystery

Angels Around Us
—Inspiring true stories about angels

Ordering Information

To order L. C. Hayden's mysteries, please visit your favorite bookstore. If the books are not on the shelves, the bookstore will order them for you at no extra charge.

Retail and wholesale customers may also order directly from the publisher by phone (972-490-9686), via www.toppub.com or you may email Lisa at lisa@toppub.com. Credit cards are accepted.

Printed in the United States
1341700001B/187-195